Music Minus One

VOCALS

SING 8 FAVORITES WITH SOUND-ALIKE DEMO & BACKING TRACKS ONLINE

RODGERS AND HAMMERSTEIN™

THE SOUND OF MUSIC®

PLAYBACK+
Speed • Pitch • Balance • Loop

To access audio visit:
www.halleonard.com/mylibrary

Enter Code
5163-4313-2526-1980

ISBN 978-1-5400-3273-7

WILLIAMSON MUSIC®
The Rodgers & Hammerstein Organization:
A Concord Music Company
www.rnh.com

EXCLUSIVELY DISTRIBUTED BY

Visit Hal Leonard Online at
www.halleonard.com

Contact Us:
Hal Leonard
7777 West Bluemound Road
Milwaukee, WI 53213
Email: info@halleonard.com

In Europe contact:
Hal Leonard Europe Limited
Distribution Centre, Newmarket Road
Bury St Edmunds, Suffolk, IP33 3YB
Email: info@halleonardeurope.com

In Australia contact:
Hal Leonard Australia Pty. Ltd.
4 Lentara Court
Cheltenham, Victoria, 3192 Australia
Email: info@halleonard.com.au

THE LONELY GOATHERD

Lyrics by OSCAR HAMMERSTEIN II
Music by RICHARD RODGERS

MARIA:

High on a hill was a lone-ly goat-herd, Lay-ee o-dl, lay-ee o-dl,
prince on the bridge of a cas-tle moat, heard Lay-ee o-dl, lay-ee o-dl,

lay-ee oo. Loud was the voice of the lone-ly goat-herd,
lay-ee oo. Men on a road, with a load to tote, heard

Lay-ee o-dl, lay-ee o-dl oo. Folks in a town that was quite re-mote, heard
Lay-ee o-dl, lay-ee o-dl oo. Men, in the midst of a ta-ble d'hôte, heard

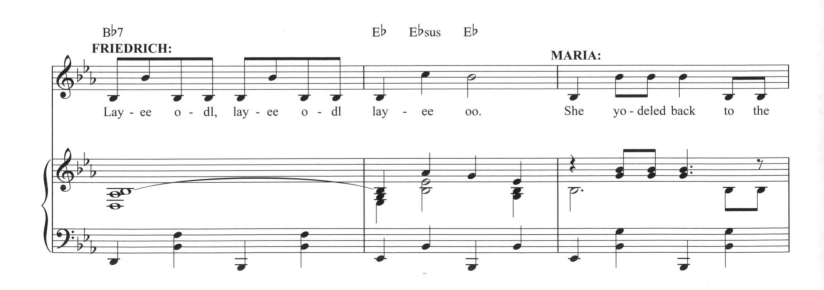

CLIMB EV'RY MOUNTAIN

Lyrics by OSCAR HAMMERSTEIN II
Music by RICHARD RODGERS

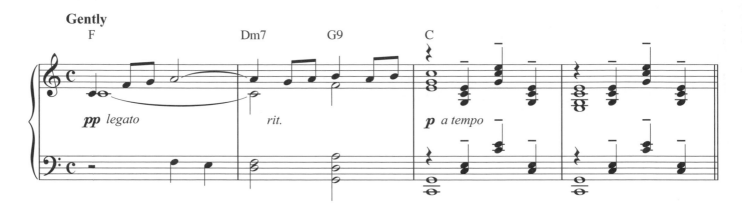

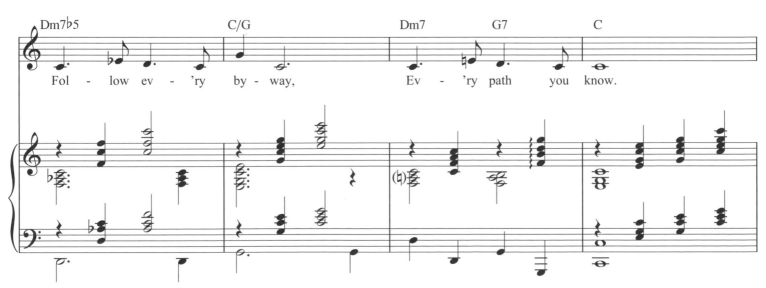

day of your life for as long as you live.

Poco pesante

Climb ev - 'ry moun - tain, Ford ev - 'ry stream.

Fol - low ev - 'ry rain - bow Till you find your

dream.

DO-RE-MI

Lyrics by OSCAR HAMMERSTEIN II
Music by RICHARD RODGERS

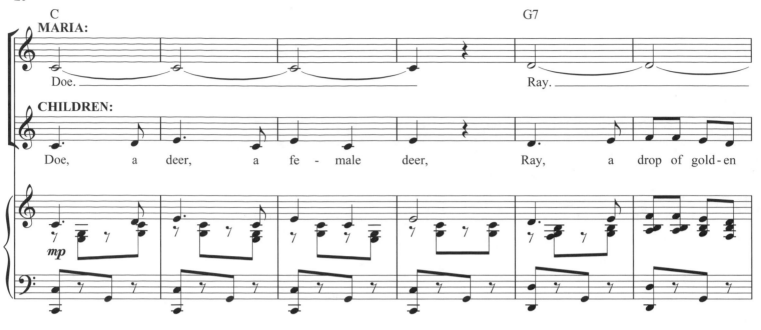

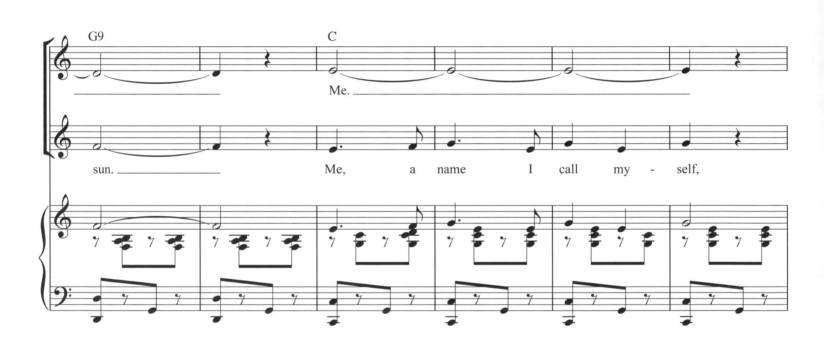

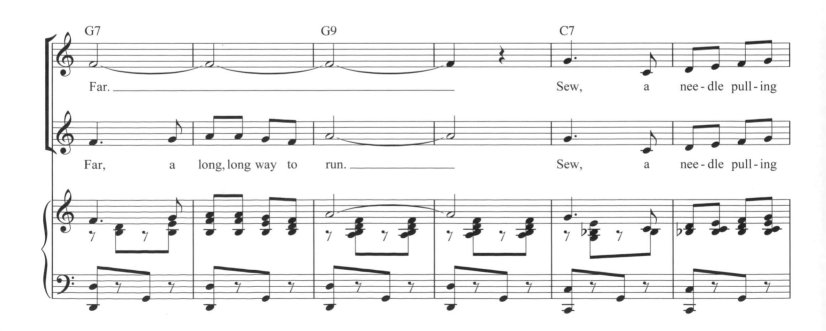

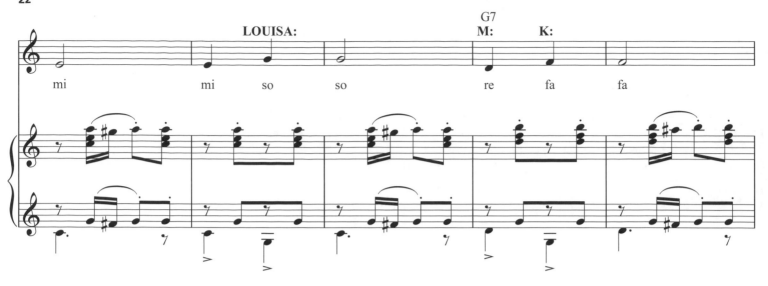

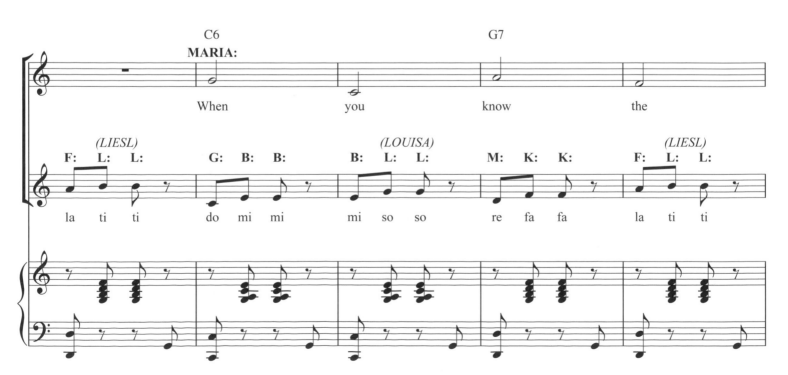

Tempo di Marcia

EDELWEISS

Lyrics by OSCAR HAMMERSTEIN II
Music by RICHARD RODGERS

MARIA

Lyrics by OSCAR HAMMERSTEIN II
Music by RICHARD RODGERS

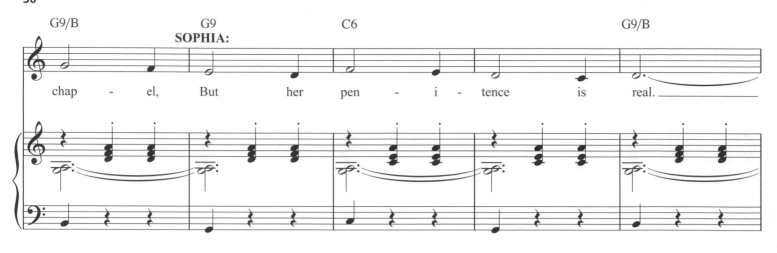

SOPHIA:

chap - el, But her pen - i - tence is real. ____

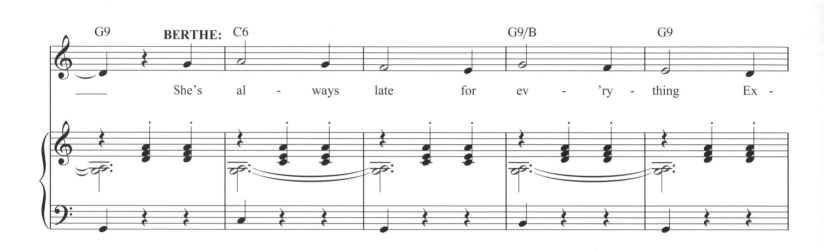

BERTHE: She's al - ways late for ev - 'ry - thing Ex -

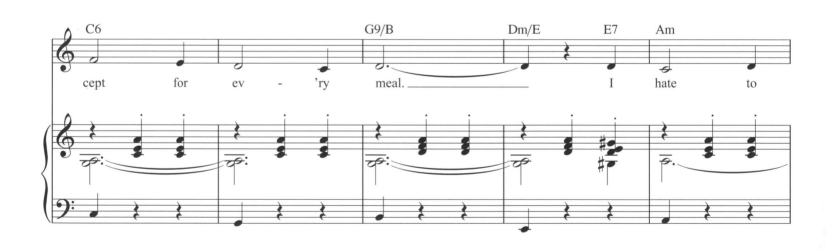

cept for ev - 'ry meal. ____ I hate to

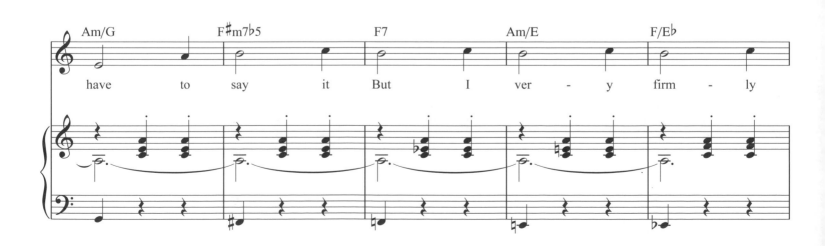

have to say it But I ver - y firm - ly

with her I'm con- fused, Out of fo- cus and be- mused, And I nev- er know ex-

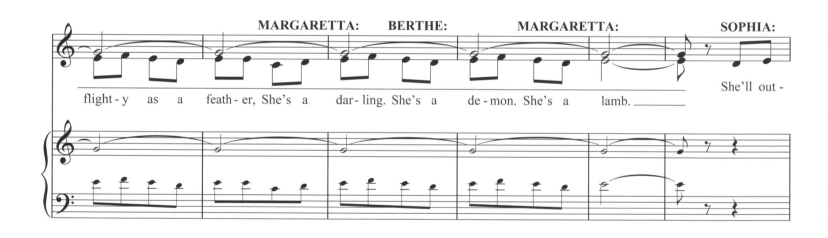

act- ly where I am. _____

BERTHE: Un- pre- dict- a- ble as weath- er, She's as

MARGARETTA: **BERTHE:** **MARGARETTA:** **SOPHIA:**

flight- y as a feath- er, She's a dar- ling. She's a de- mon. She's a lamb. _____ She'll out-

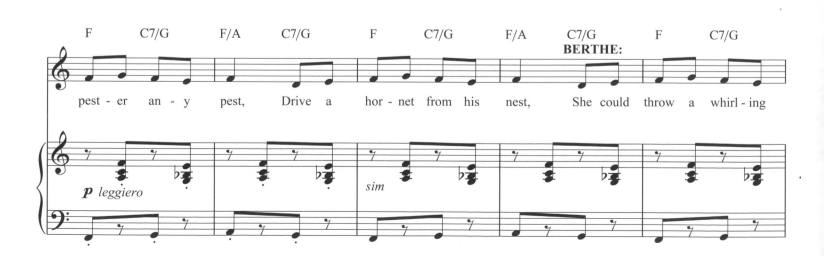

F   C7/G   F/A   C7/G   F   C7/G   F/A   C7/G   F   C7/G

BERTHE:

pest- er an- y pest, Drive a hor- net from his nest, She could throw a whirl- ing

MY FAVORITE THINGS

Lyrics by OSCAR HAMMERSTEIN II
Music by RICHARD RODGERS

Girls in white dress - es with blue sat - in sash - es,

snow - flakes that stay on my nose and eye - lash - es, sil - ver white

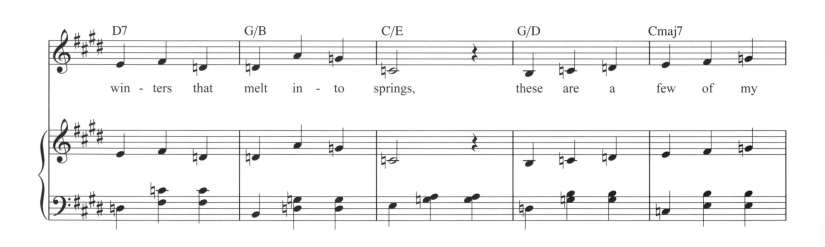

win - ters that melt in - to springs, these are a few of my

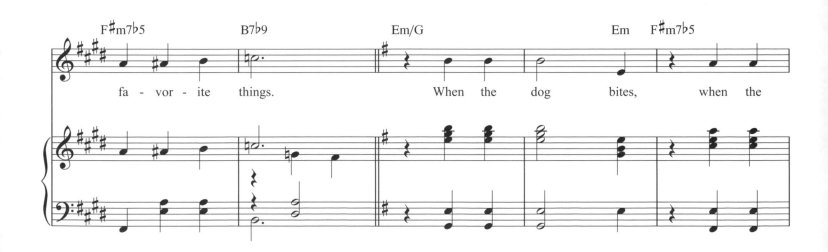

fa - vor - ite things. When the dog bites, when the

bee stings, when I'm feel - ing sad,   I

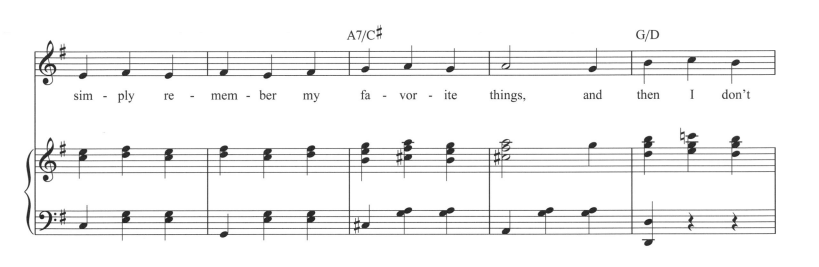

sim - ply re - mem - ber my fa - vor - ite things, and then I don't

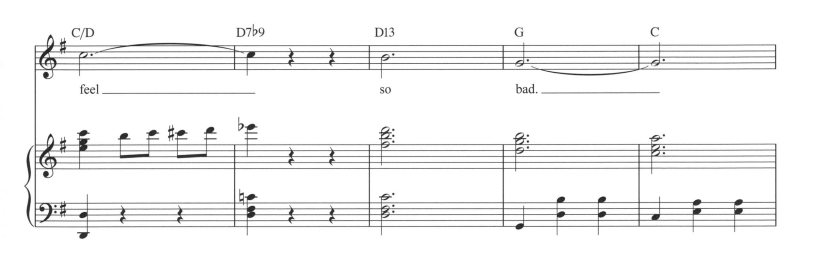

feel _____ so   bad. _____

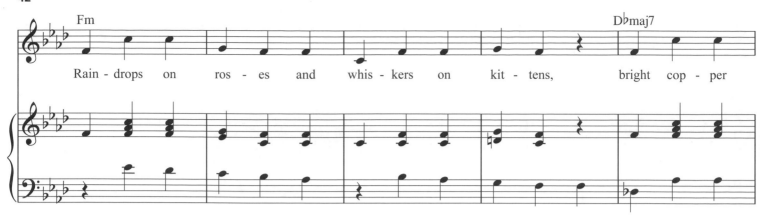

Rain - drops on ros - es and whis - kers on kit - tens, bright cop - per

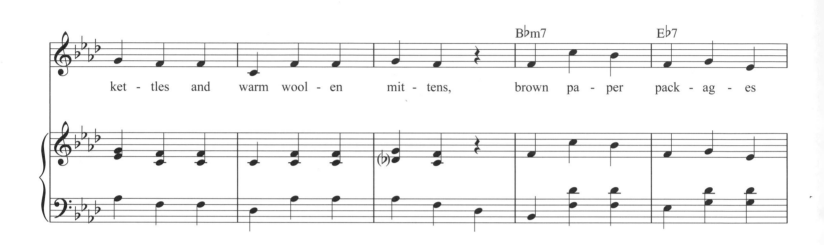

ket - tles and warm wool - en mit - tens, brown pa - per pack - ag - es

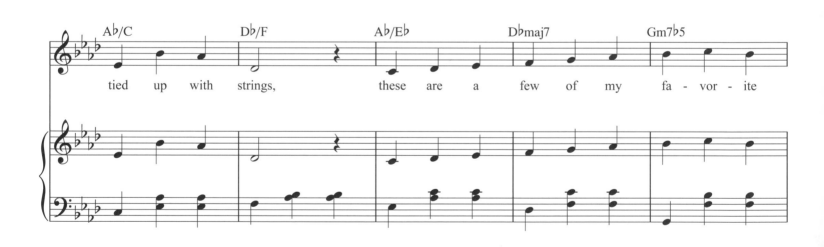

tied up with strings, these are a few of my fa - vor - ite

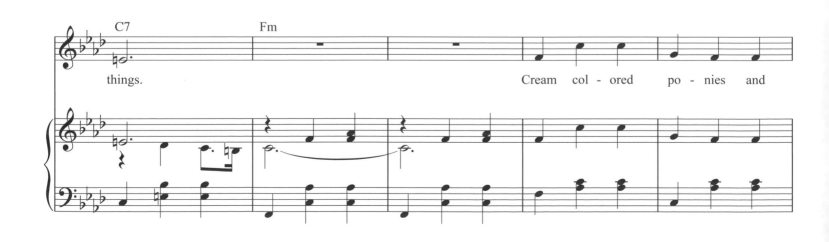

things. Cream col - ored po - nies and

crisp ap - ple stru - dels, door - bells and sleigh - bells and schnit - zel with

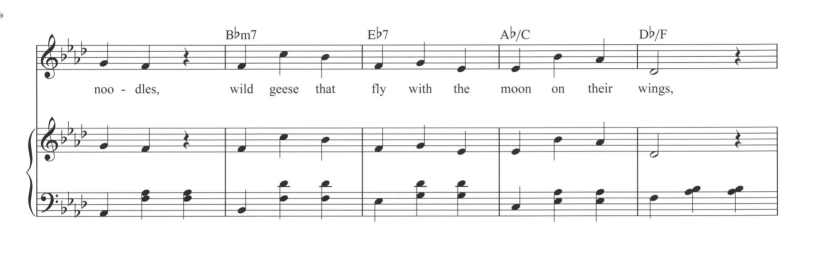

noo - dles, wild geese that fly with the moon on their wings,

these are a few of my fa - vor - ite things.

Girls in white dress - es with blue sat - in

sash - es, snow - flakes that stay on my nose and eye - lash - es,

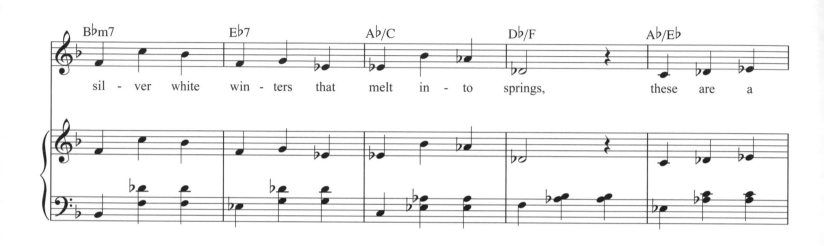

sil - ver white win - ters that melt in - to springs, these are a

few of my fa - vor - ite things. When the

dog bites, when the bee stings, when I'm feel - ing

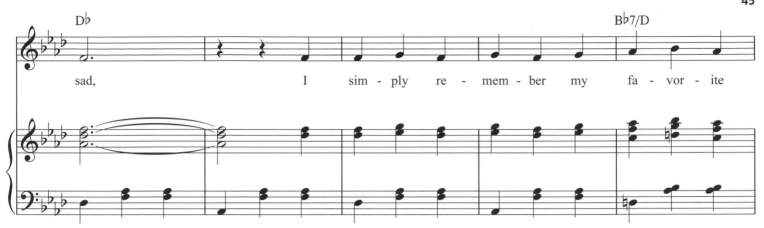

sad, I sim - ply re - mem - ber my fa - vor - ite

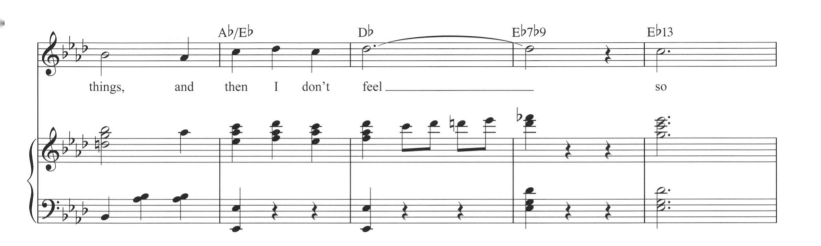

things, and then I don't feel _____ so

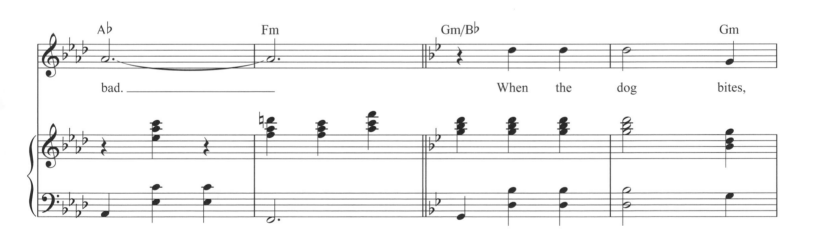

bad. _____ When the dog bites,

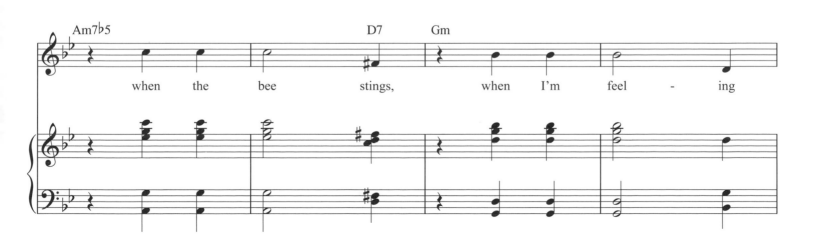

when the bee stings, when I'm feel - ing

sad, _____ I sim - ply re - mem - ber my

fa - vor - ite things, and then I don't feel _____

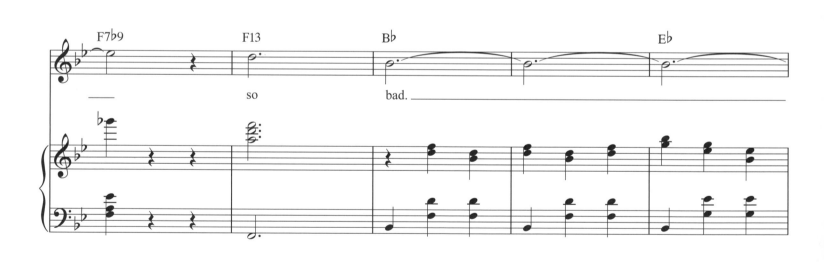

___ so bad. _____

SIXTEEN GOING ON SEVENTEEN

Lyrics by OSCAR HAMMERSTEIN II
Music by RICHARD RODGERS

THE SOUND OF MUSIC

Lyrics by OSCAR HAMMERSTEIN II
Music by RICHARD RODGERS

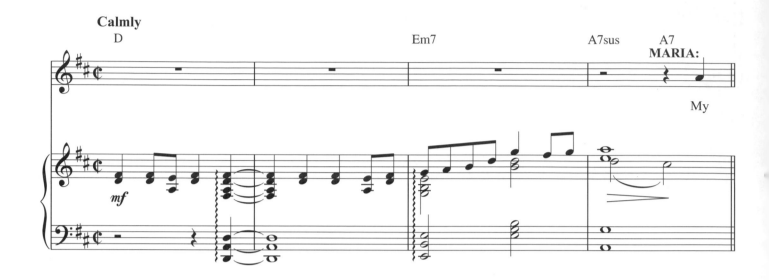

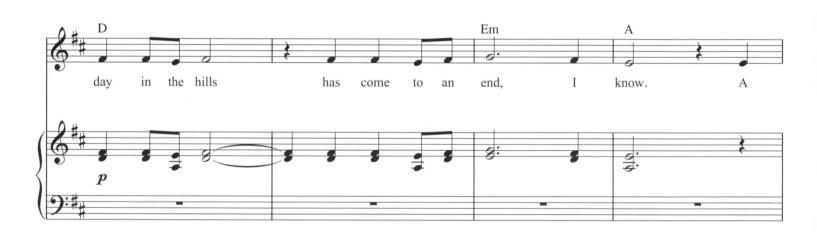

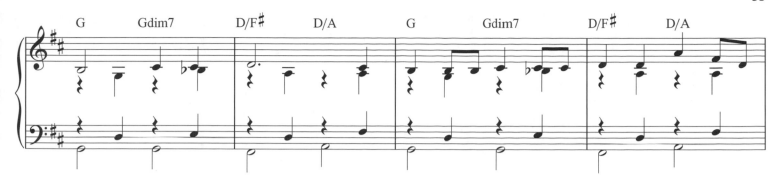

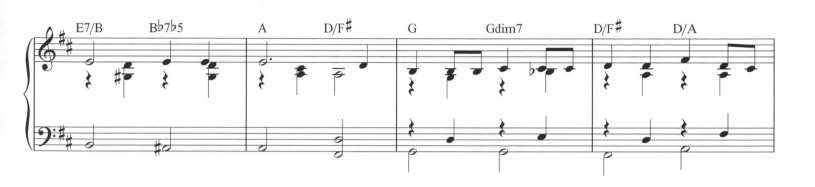

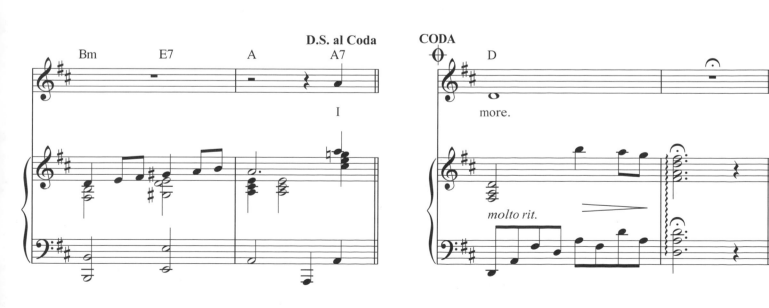

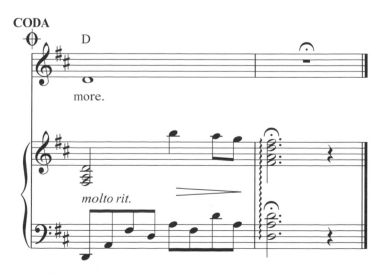